JACKIE ROBINSON

by Sally M. Walker
illustrations by Rodney S. Pate

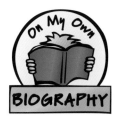

M Millbrook Press/Minneapolis

Photograph on p. 47 © Bettmann/CORBIS. Quotations reprinted from: pp. 24, 29, Carl Rowan and Jackie Robinson, *Wait Till Next Year* (New York: Random House, 1960), p. 149; p. 41, Jackie Robinson, *I Never Had It Made* (New York: G. P. Putnam and Sons, 1972), p. 73.

This book is available in two editions:
Library binding by Millbrook Press, a division of Lerner Publishing Group, Inc.
Soft cover by First Avenue Editions, an imprint of Lerner Publishing Group, Inc.
241 First Avenue North
Minneapolis, MN 55401 USA

For reading levels and more information, look up this title at www.lernerbooks.com.

Library of Congress Cataloging-in-Publication Data

Walker, Sally M.
    Jackie Robinson / by Sally M. Walker ; illustrations by Rodney S. Pate.
      p.   cm. — (On my own biography)
    Summary: Describes the life and accomplishments of baseball star Jackie Robinson, who became the first African American in twentieth-century major-league baseball.
    ISBN 978–0–87614–599–9 (lib. bdg. : alk. paper)
    ISBN 978–0–87614–904–1 (pbk. : alk. paper)
    ISBN 978–0–87614–042–0 (EB pdf)
    1. Robinson, Jackie, 1919–1972—Juvenile literature. 2. Baseball players—United States—Biography—Juvenile literature. 3. African American baseball players—Biography—Juvenile literature. [1. Robinson, Jackie, 1919–1972. 2. Baseball players. 3. African Americans—Biography.] I. Pate, Rodney S., ill. II. Title. III. Series.
GV865.R6 W35 2002
796.357'092—dc21   2001006584

Manufactured in the United States of America
16-50711-6293-4/22/2021

*For Allen "Pea-head" Walker, the family's third baseman.
And in memory of William "Grandpa" Inge, who once
served as Ty Cobb's batboy — S. M. W.*

*To my nephew Andrew—may you grow to be as strong as
Jackie. Also to J. F. and B. G. — R. S. P.*

Pepper Street

Pasadena, California, 1927

THUNK!

A rock hit the ground at eight-year-old
Jackie Robinson's feet.

He picked it up and threw it right back.

The white man across the street was angry.

Jackie was angry, too.

The man's daughter had called Jackie
a terrible name.

Jackie was sick and tired of being
picked on because he was black.

So he had yelled at the girl.

That's when the rock throwing started.

It wasn't easy being the only
black family on the block.
Many white people on Pepper Street
did not want the Robinsons around.
Some even called the police when Jackie
and his brothers played outside.
At least the kids on Pepper Street
liked to play sports.
Jackie fit right in when a game began.
He played soccer, football, handball,
baseball, and dodgeball.
He played every game well—very well.
Jackie loved to win,
and he almost always did.

Jackie's mother, Mallie, worked hard
to make a good home for her children.
She told them to be proud of their race.
The neighbors would accept them with time.
Meanwhile, her family would set
a good example.
The Robinsons didn't have much money.
But whenever Mallie had extra food,
she shared it with her neighbors.
She even shared with the man
who had thrown rocks at Jackie.
She told Jackie and his brothers to help
their neighbors do chores—for free.
It took several years, but Mallie was right.
The neighbors became friendlier.
Jackie realized that skin color mattered less
when people got to know each other.

As Jackie grew up,

he got even better at sports.

At Pasadena Junior College,

he was the best scorer in basketball.

In track, he smashed his brother Mack's

record in the broad jump.

In baseball games, he stole bases

in the blink of an eye.

He starred in every sport he played.
Most of Jackie's teammates were white.
A few did not like playing
with a black athlete.
Jackie treated them with respect anyway.
Over time, his teammates saw that
he played fairly and well.
Most of them came to respect him, too.

Teams from other towns were different.
Sometimes white players said nasty things
about black people to Jackie.
Their insults made Jackie angry.
Usually he just played harder.
But sometimes he got into fights.
Even in Pasadena, the rules weren't fair
off the playing field.
Black people could swim in the
town's pool only on Tuesdays.
Some restaurants would not serve
black customers.
Jackie hated this kind of unfairness.
Sometimes his anger got him into trouble.
One time, he argued with a white policeman.
Jackie had to spend the night in jail.
Some people started saying that
Jackie Robinson was a troublemaker.

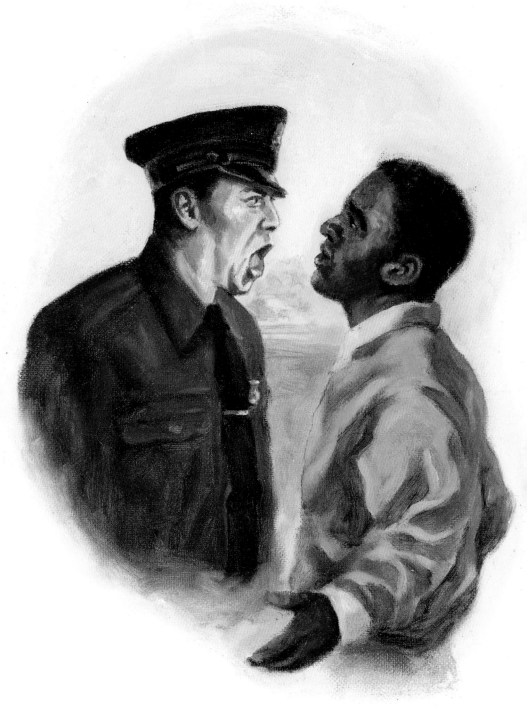

Then a man named Karl Downs
came into Jackie's life.

He was the new minister of Mallie's church.

Reverend Downs listened when Jackie talked
about his problems.

He helped Jackie set goals.

Jackie joined church clubs, too.
Mallie had always found strength
in her belief in God.
Soon Jackie did as well.
His faith helped him think twice
before he lost his temper.

15

From Pasadena, Jackie went on to the
University of California in Los Angeles.
There he fell in love with Rachel Isum.
She was friendly and smart.
Jackie liked how she said what she thought,
even when she disagreed with him.
They began to see each other often.
Jackie had to join the army
during World War II.
He served from 1942 to 1944.
When he left the army, he wasn't sure
what the future would bring.
He was sure of two things, though.
He wanted to find a job in sports.
And he wanted to marry Rachel.
Maybe he could find a way to do both.

Baseball Star
Kansas City, 1945

Jackie watched the pitcher wind up.

A curve ball zoomed toward home plate.

It might have fooled some hitters,

but not Jackie Robinson.

C-R-A-C-K!

The ball soared into the outfield.

A base hit!

At age 26, Jackie had found a job
playing a sport he loved.
He had joined the Kansas City Monarchs,
a team in the Negro American League.
Black athletes had not been allowed to play
major-league baseball since 1884.
They could only play in the Negro leagues.
The Monarchs had many outstanding players.
Jackie learned all he could from them.

The Negro leagues were far from perfect.

Road trips were tough.

White hotel owners would not rent rooms
to the Monarchs.

They had to sleep in the bus.

And white gas station owners didn't let
the team use their restrooms.

Jackie's old anger came back.

Sometimes he thought about quitting.

Then Jackie got a surprise.

In August of 1945, Branch Rickey

invited Jackie to meet him.

Rickey was the president of New York's

famous Brooklyn Dodgers.

Like all major-league teams,

the Dodgers were all white.

Why would Rickey want to see Jackie?

The two men met secretly in New York City.

Rickey made a stunning offer.

He wanted Jackie to play

for the Montreal Royals in Canada.

The Royals were the Dodgers' training team.

If Jackie played well enough,

he would move up to the Dodgers.

Jackie could not speak.

Was it possible that he might get to play

major-league baseball?

Branch Rickey had more to say.

All black athletes would be judged

by what Jackie did and said.

His success would depend on how well

he could control his temper.

Some people would be cruel.

They would try to get Jackie to yell or fight.

Rickey needed "a ball player with

guts enough not to fight back."

He tested Jackie to show what he meant.

Rickey pretended to be a white player

who hated black people.

He shouted insults about Jackie's race

and his family.

Those things were hard to listen to.

But Jackie kept his mouth shut.

Then he promised to do as Rickey asked.

No matter what others did,

Jackie would not shout or start a fight.

The two men shook hands.

Jackie Robinson was going to Montreal.

Jackie would not have to start
his new life alone.
In February of 1946, he married Rachel.
Soon he had his first test at
holding his temper.
On the way to Florida for spring training,
he and Rachel lost their places
on their flight.
White people wanted their seats.

26

Then the Robinsons could not
find a hotel for blacks.
To complete their trip, they were forced
to sit at the back of a bus.
Jackie was furious, but he
remembered his promise.
He hid his anger as well as he could.
He knew that this trip was
just the beginning.

Royal Talent

Jersey City, New Jersey, April 18, 1946

Opening day!

Jackie's heart pounded.

His stomach felt like it was "full of feverish

fireflies with claws on their feet."

The crowd in Roosevelt Stadium

was excited, too.

They wanted to see what the black player

at second base could do.

Jackie showed them.

His second time at bat, he slammed

the ball into the left-field stands.

A three-run homer!

By the end of the game,

Jackie had four hits and four runs.

The Royals beat Jersey City, 14 to 1.

Jackie's sharp game made him
a favorite of the Montreal fans.
In Canada, most people didn't care
what color his skin was.
They just loved the way he played.
But games in the United States
weren't so easy.

Thousands of black fans cheered for Jackie.

Many white fans did, too.

But others screamed crude insults.

Players from other teams taunted him.

Pitchers sometimes even threw the ball
at him on purpose.

Jackie had to take it all in silence.

That first season was not easy.

But by the end, Jackie had made his mark.

He drove in 66 runs and scored 113.

He stole 40 bases.

He was the league's best batter that year.

The Royals won the 1946 Little World Series.

And Jackie had not lost his temper once.

Jackie was happy to have played so well.

In November, he felt even happier.

Rachel gave birth to a son.

Jackie hoped that Jackie Junior would see him play in the major leagues.

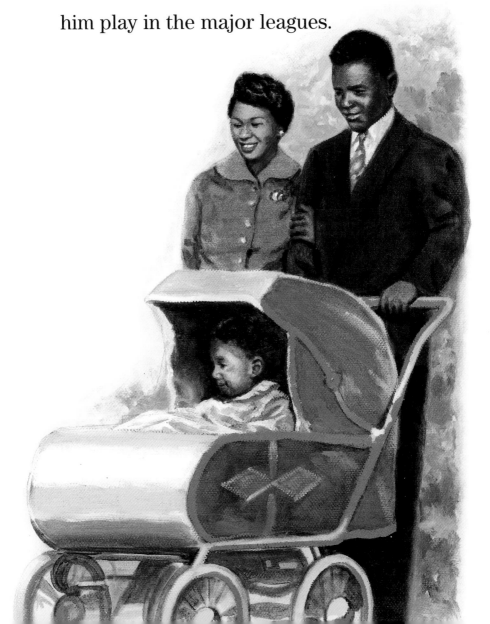

The Major Leagues
Brooklyn, New York, April 11, 1947

Jackie looked up at the crowd.

He could hardly believe it.

He was a real Brooklyn Dodger—

number 42, playing first base.

The Dodgers were up against the New York

Yankees in a pre-season game.

Jackie pounded his fist into his glove

and leaned forward.

He would be ready if the ball came his way.

Jackie didn't get any hits in that game,

but he drove in three runs.

Winning the game was easy enough.

Winning the support of some of his

new teammates was not.

A few made rude comments.

Others kept open minds.

Eddie Stanky and Pee Wee Reese
were helpful.
They gave Jackie tips on how to improve
his skills at first base.
Jackie worked hard at practice.
He would do his best for his new team.

The season opened on April 15.

Jackie received letters full of hatred.

Some people threatened to kill him

or hurt his family if he kept playing.

Jackie heard plenty of insults

on the playing field, too.

He tried to remember Mallie's lesson

back on Pepper Street.

People needed time to get used to change.

Jackie kept his promise to Branch Rickey.

He didn't fight back.

He didn't even show how terrible

he felt inside.

On April 22, the Dodgers
played the Philadelphia Phillies.
The Phillies' insults were the worst yet.
Jackie thought he would explode.
Then his teammate Eddie Stanky
started yelling.

"Listen, you yellow-bellied cowards,"
he shouted at the Phillies.
"Why don't you yell at somebody
who can answer back?"
Jackie realized that he wasn't alone.
He clenched his teeth and hung on.

Slowly, Jackie's new teammates
got to know him.
Once he felt more at home,
he caught fire on the playing field.
His bat blasted out base hits.
He stole base after base, even home plate.
The fans loved him for his daring.

Jackie's rookie season was a great one.
He led the National League in stolen bases.
He scored 125 runs.
The *Sporting News* named him
the 1947 Rookie of the Year.
No one could ever again say that
a black man was not good enough
to play major-league baseball.

The next year, in August,
Jackie finally lost his temper.
But it wasn't about insults.
The umpire threw one of the Dodgers
out of a game.
Jackie got mad.
He stormed out of the dugout, shouting.
The umpire threw him out, too.

Jackie could tell that it wasn't
because he was black.
Yelling at the umpire is against the rules.
The umpire had simply treated Jackie
like any other ball player.
After all Jackie had been through,
that felt just fine.
Even better, it felt *fair*.

Jackie knew that his hard times in
baseball were not over.
American sports still had a long way to go
to become truly fair to all players.
But thanks to Jackie
and those who helped him,
the days when race was more important
than skills were gone for good.

Afterword

Jackie played for the Brooklyn Dodgers for 10 years, mostly at second base. Many other courageous athletes joined the struggle to make baseball open to players of all races. They included Larry Doby, Roy Campanella, and Satchel Paige.

Jackie's many honors as a Dodger included being named the National League's Most Valuable Player in 1949. When he retired from baseball, he worked in business and became active in the civil rights movement. In 1962, he became the first African American to be inducted into the Baseball Hall of Fame.

Jackie Robinson died in 1972 at the age of 53. It was not until 1975 that a black man, Frank Robinson of the Cleveland Indians, finally became a major-league team manager. As in many areas of American life, people are still working toward equal treatment for all in sports.

Important Dates

1919—Jack Roosevelt Robinson was born near Cairo, Georgia, on January 31.

1920—Family moved to Pasadena, California

1937—Began attending Pasadena Junior College

1939—Began attending University of California-Los Angeles

1942—Joined United States army; served until 1944

1945—Joined and played for Kansas City Monarchs; met Branch Rickey; joined Montreal Royals

1946—Married Rachel Isum; played for Montreal Royals; birth of son, Jackie Junior, first of three children

1947—Began playing for Brooklyn Dodgers as first black major-league player since 1884

1949—Named National League's Most Valuable Player

1957—Retired from baseball

1962—Inducted into Baseball Hall of Fame

1972—Dodgers retired his number, 42, meaning that no other Dodger could wear it. Robinson died on October 24 in Stamford, Connecticut.

1984—Awarded the Presidential Medal of Freedom, the United States' highest award for non-military achievement, by President Ronald Reagan

1997—Number 42 retired from use by all major-league baseball teams